# An Alphabet of Farm Animals

*Mary Griese*

by

Mary Griese

© Mary Griese, 2014

Published by
Mary Griese, 2014

All rights reserved. No part of this book may be reproduced in any material form (including photocopying or storing it in any medium by electronic means and whether or not transiently or incidentally to some other use of this publication) without the written permission of the copyright owner.

ISBN 978 0 9930851 0 9

Printed by
Dinefwr Press, Rawlings Road, Llandybie, Carmarthenshire

Mary Griese was born in Bath and studied at the West of England College of Art. Both her Welsh father and maternal Irish/Yorkshire grandfather were artists. For most of her adult life she has managed to combine art with farming and writing.

In 1987, while sheep farming on the Black Mountain in South Wales, she set up 'Slightly Sheepish', a range of greetings cards and prints from her watercolours of farm livestock. She sells her work at agricultural shows and sheepdog trials, provides designs for various sheep and cattle breed societies, takes private commissions of prize livestock and has illustrated several books.

Mary now lives in Somerset. She has two children and two grandchildren.

## Author's Note

When I was a little girl it was a special bedtime treat to look at *A Child's Book of Natural History*. My father turned the pages, which were edged in what I thought to be pure gold and my favourite illustration was of a polar bear in a dark mysterious background. The book was my father's sixth birthday present, which makes it almost a hundred years old.

   I hope this alphabet book might become such a treasure.

Dinefwr Press printed my first cards. I'm delighted they are producing my book, not only for their quality printing, but also as a tribute to Donald Martin, who was always hugely supportive of Slightly Sheepish. Thank you to Clive Arnold of Phoenix Fine Art Prints for his invaluable input and meticulous scanning of my paintings and to my family and friends for their encouragement.

My pages are numbered on the left hand side only, to indicate the place of each letter in the alphabet.

   In a montage of animals work clockwise from top left.

*For Charlie and Molly,
my darlings.*

**Aberdeen Angus and Ayrshires amble along amicably.**

**b**eautiful **B**eulah

**bi**g **b**arn

**b**ashful **B**luefaced Leicester

**b**onny **B**alwen

**b**old **B**order Leicester

**bi**gger **b**arn

**b**eguiling **B**adger Face

**B**lue Texel **b**a**b**ies

**b**est **B**lack Welsh Mountain

**c**on**c**entrating **c**ollies
**c**harming **C**harollais sheep
**c**ream-**c**oloured **C**harolais **c**ow

**d**azzling **D**erbyshire Gritstone
**d**elightful **D**orset **D**own
**d**ear **D**exter
**d**arling **d**onkey

extraordinary **E**xmoor Horn

fresh fields for Friesians

gorgeous Greyface Dartmoor

**h**azel **h**edge
**h**airy **H**ighland
**h**appy **h**en
**h**andsome **H**aflinger
**h**igh-yielding **H**olstein
**h**eavenly **h**ay

incredibly inquisitive Indian Runners

jaunty Jerseys
jazzy Jacobs

**ki**ndly **K**erry Hill
**k**een **K**erry Hills
**ki**ss **ki**ss **K**une**k**une
**K**ha**k**i Campbells **k**eeping up

legendary Longhorn
lovable Lleyn
lustrous Limousin
little Llanwenog

**m**essy **m**uckspreader
**m**ilky **M**iddlewhite pig
**m**oon daisy **m**eadow
**m**aternal **M**ule
**m**odel **M**asha**m**s

**n**atteri**n**g **N**orth Cou**n**try Cheviots
with **n**otably **n**oble **n**oses

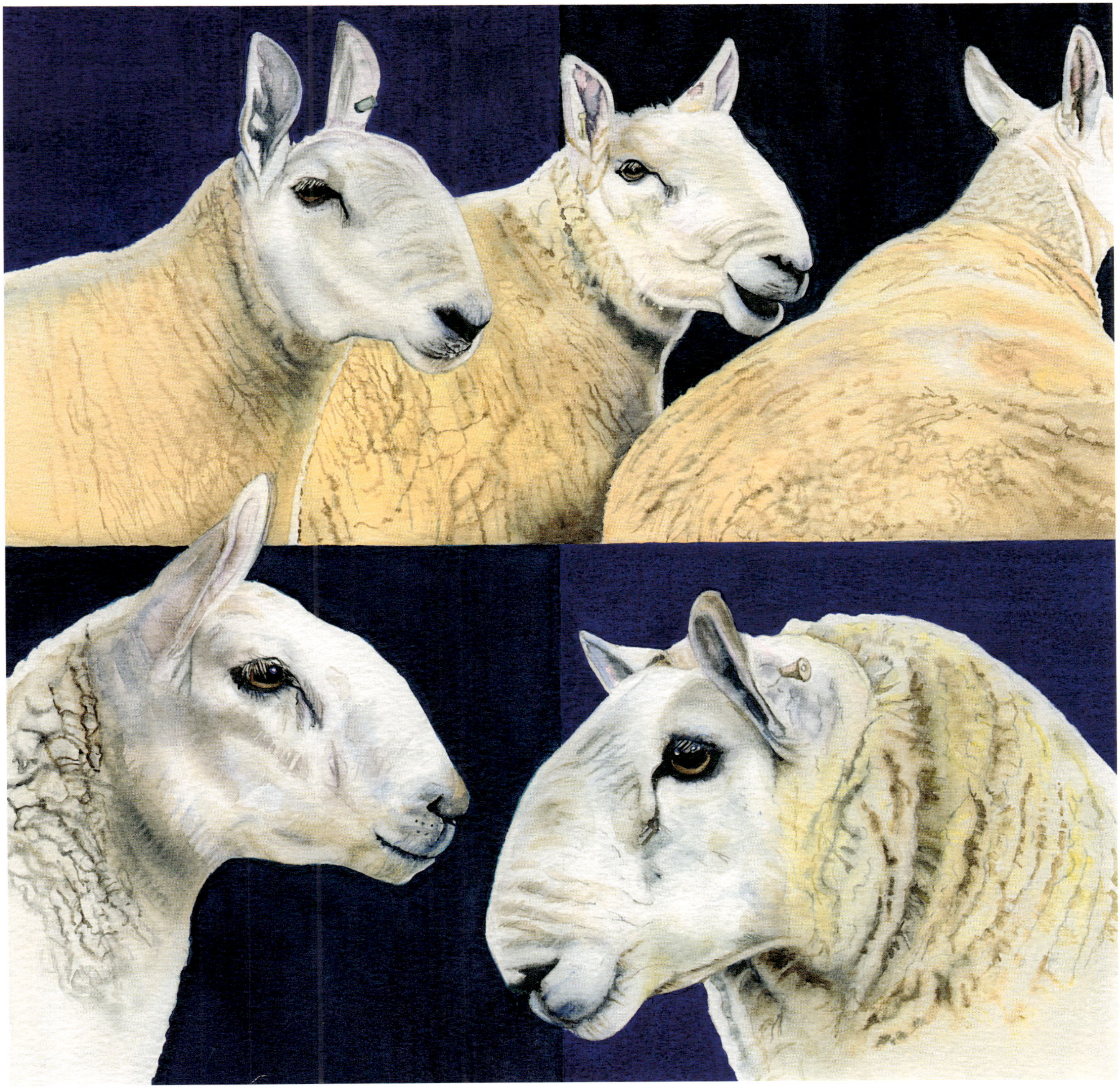

**o**ld **o**ak tree
**o**cean **of o**ilseed rape
**o**utstanding **O**xford **D**own
**o**ink **o**ink **O**xfo**r**d Sandy and Blacks

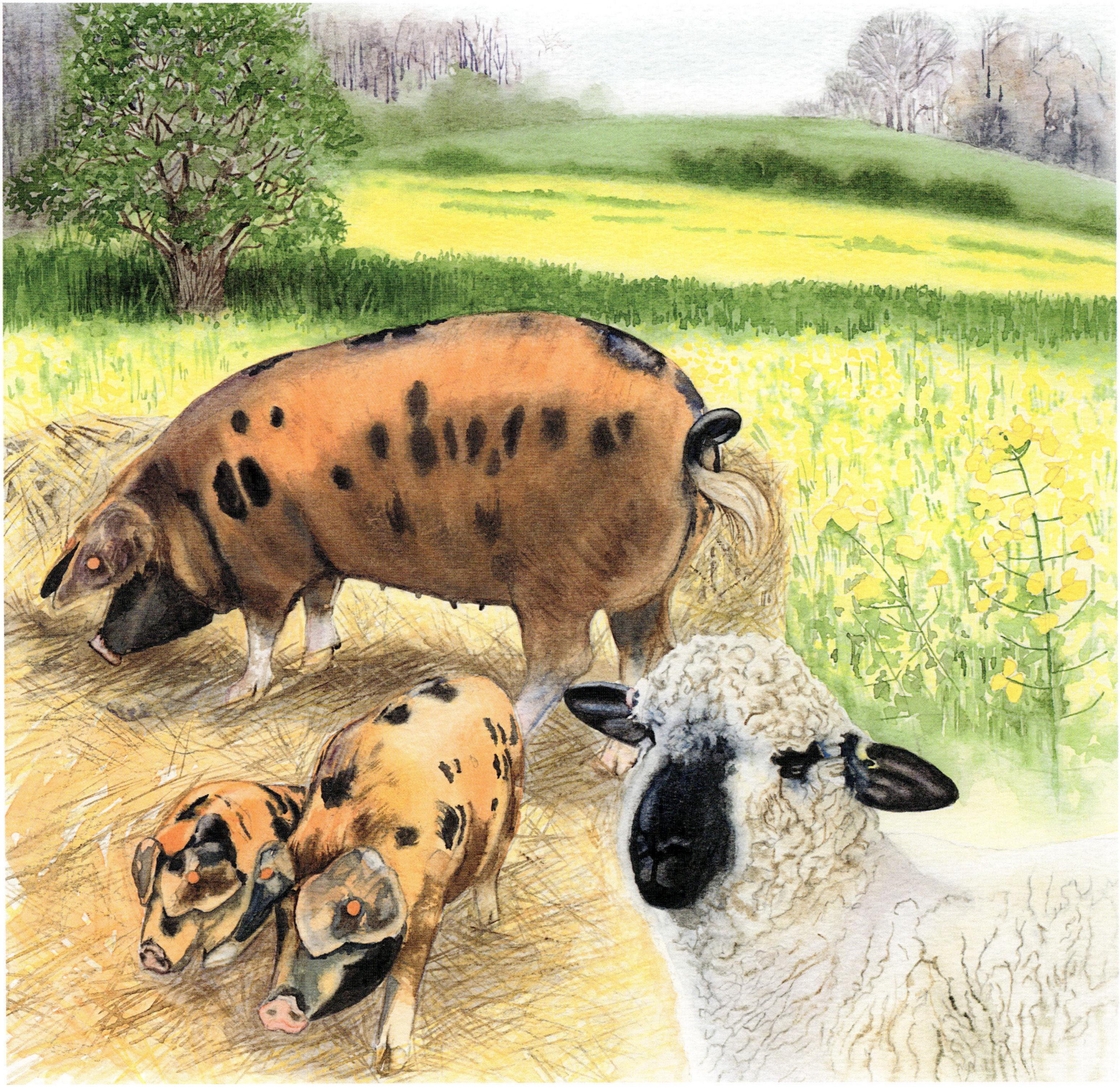

**pur**osefully **p**loughed field
**p**eaceful **P**ortland
**p**li**p p**lo**p p**uddle

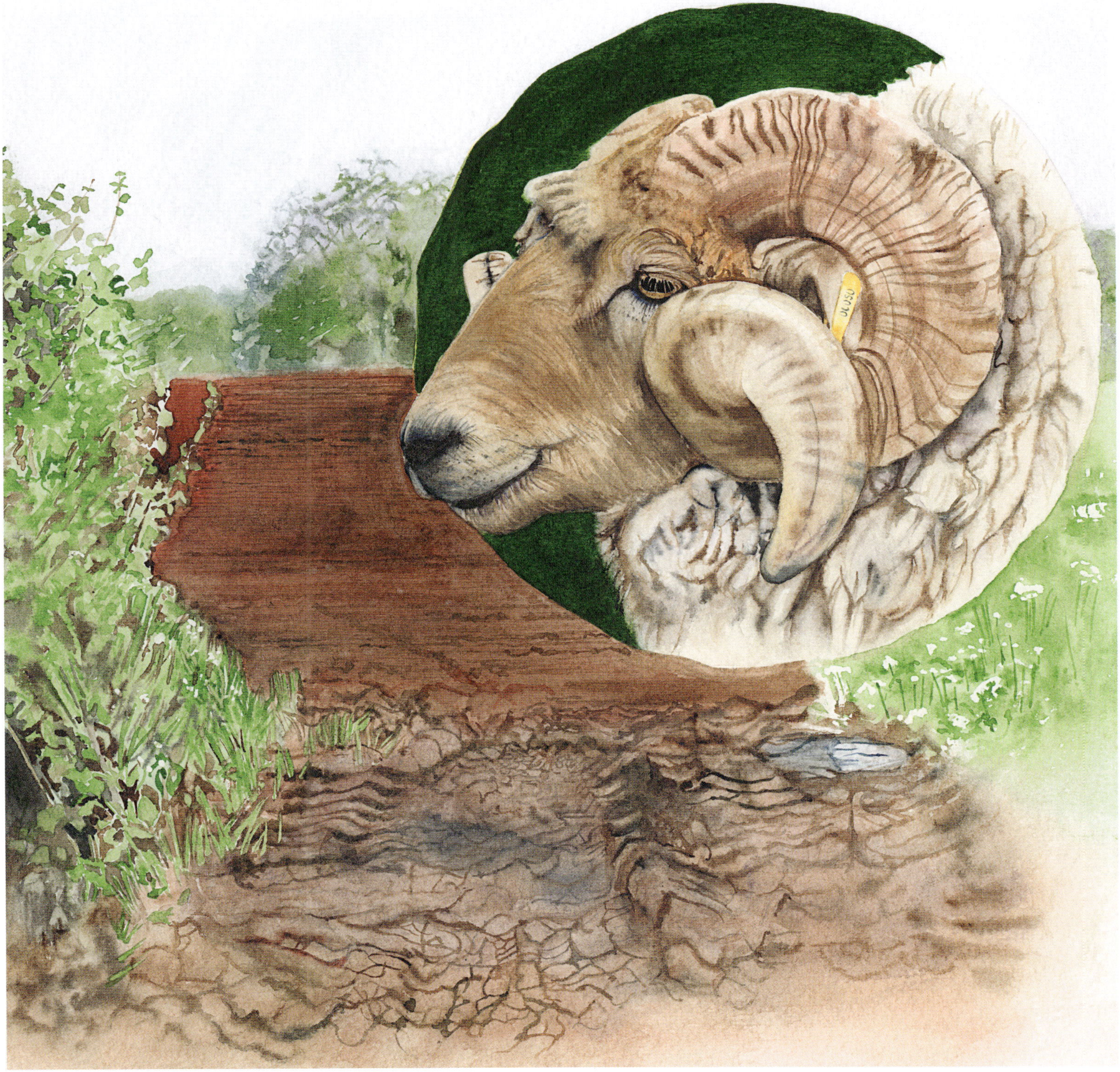

**q**uirky **q**ueen bee in **q**uad **q**ueue

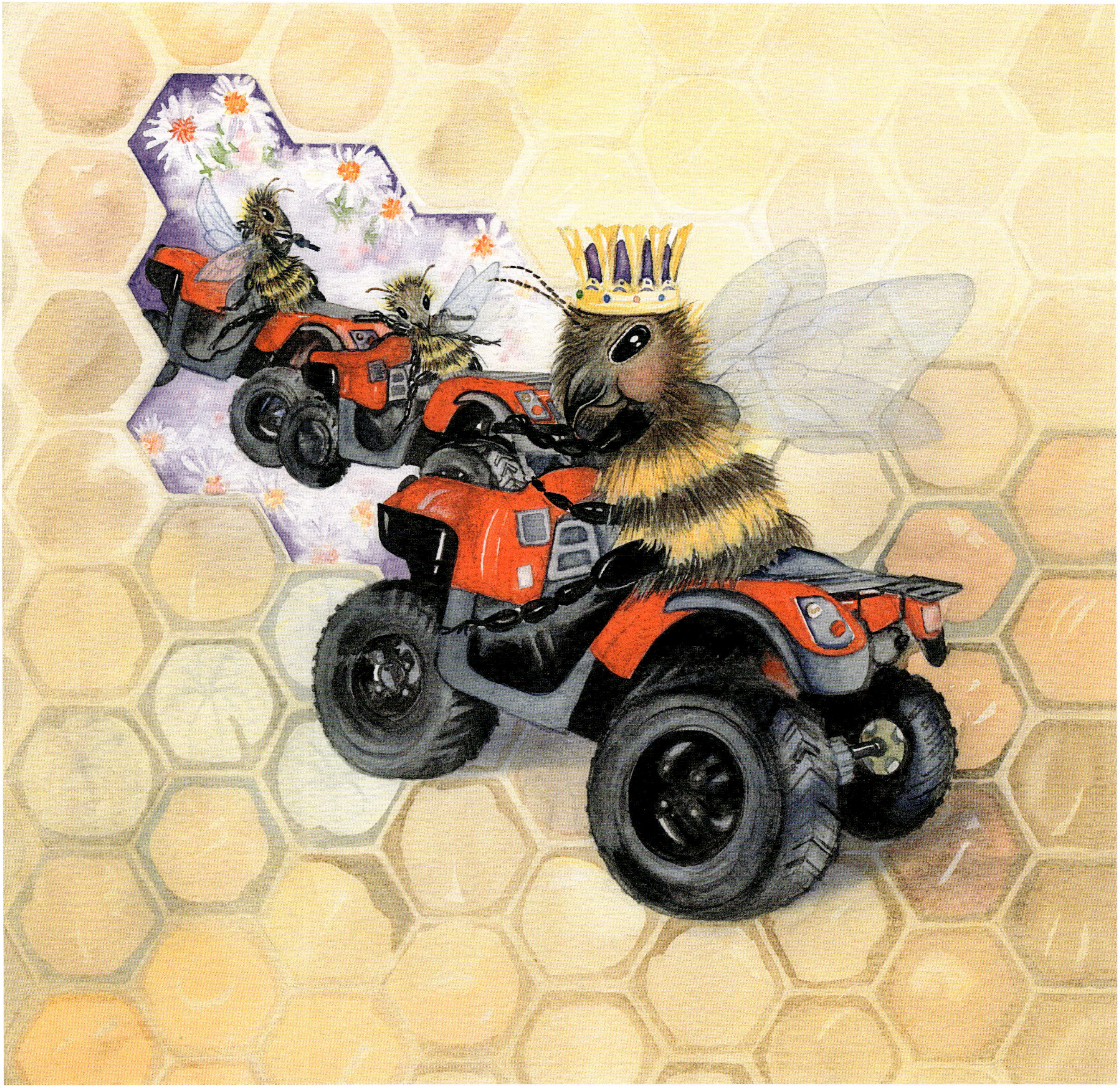

**r**obust **R**yeland
**r**adiant **R**uby **R**ed Devons
**r**ecyclable **r**aincoat
**r**avishing **R**ough Fell

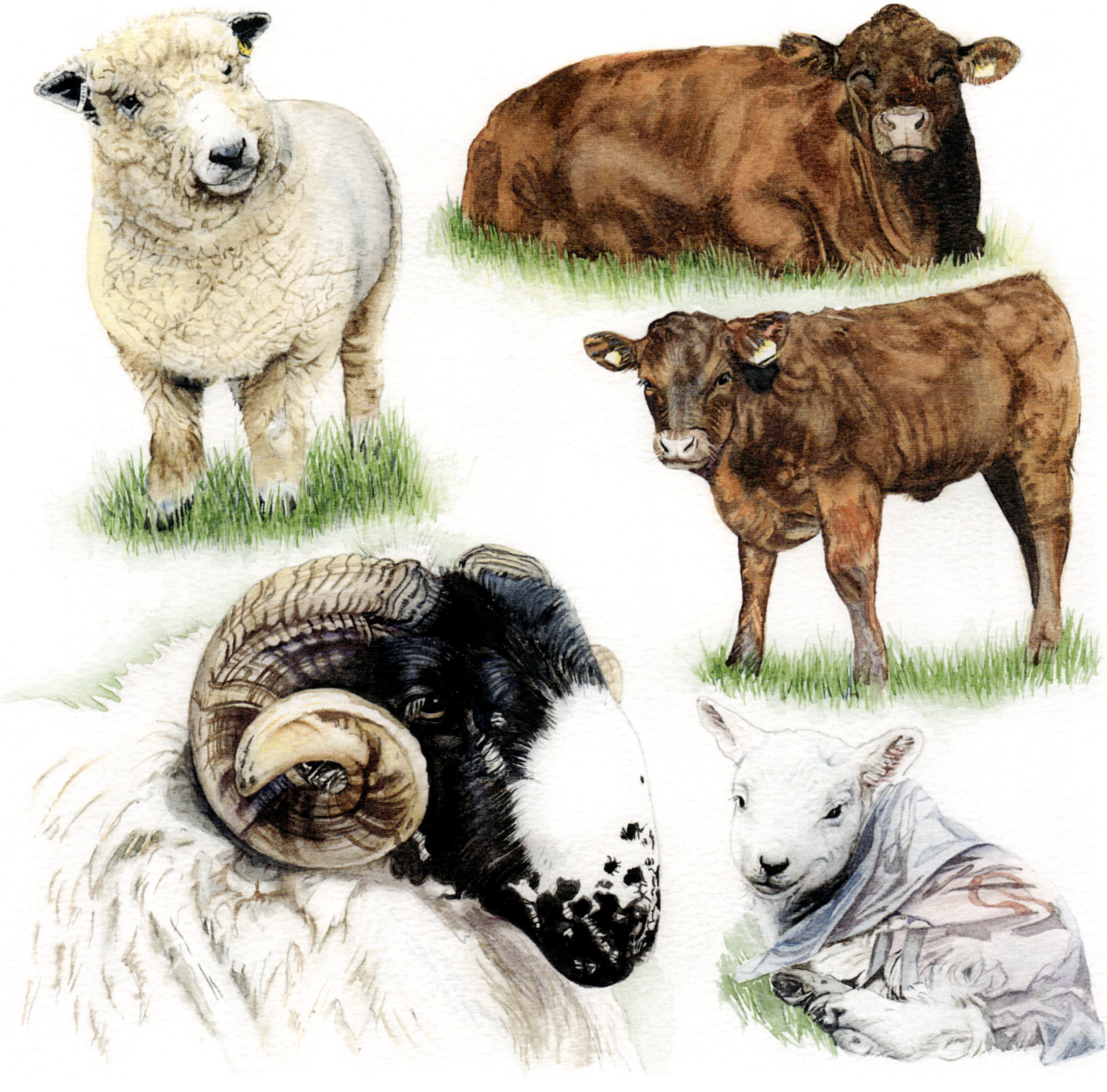

sturdy shed
seven silage bales
strong Saddleback
special Shropshire
sweetie Shetland
smart Suffolk
small Springer Spaniel
spry Swaledale

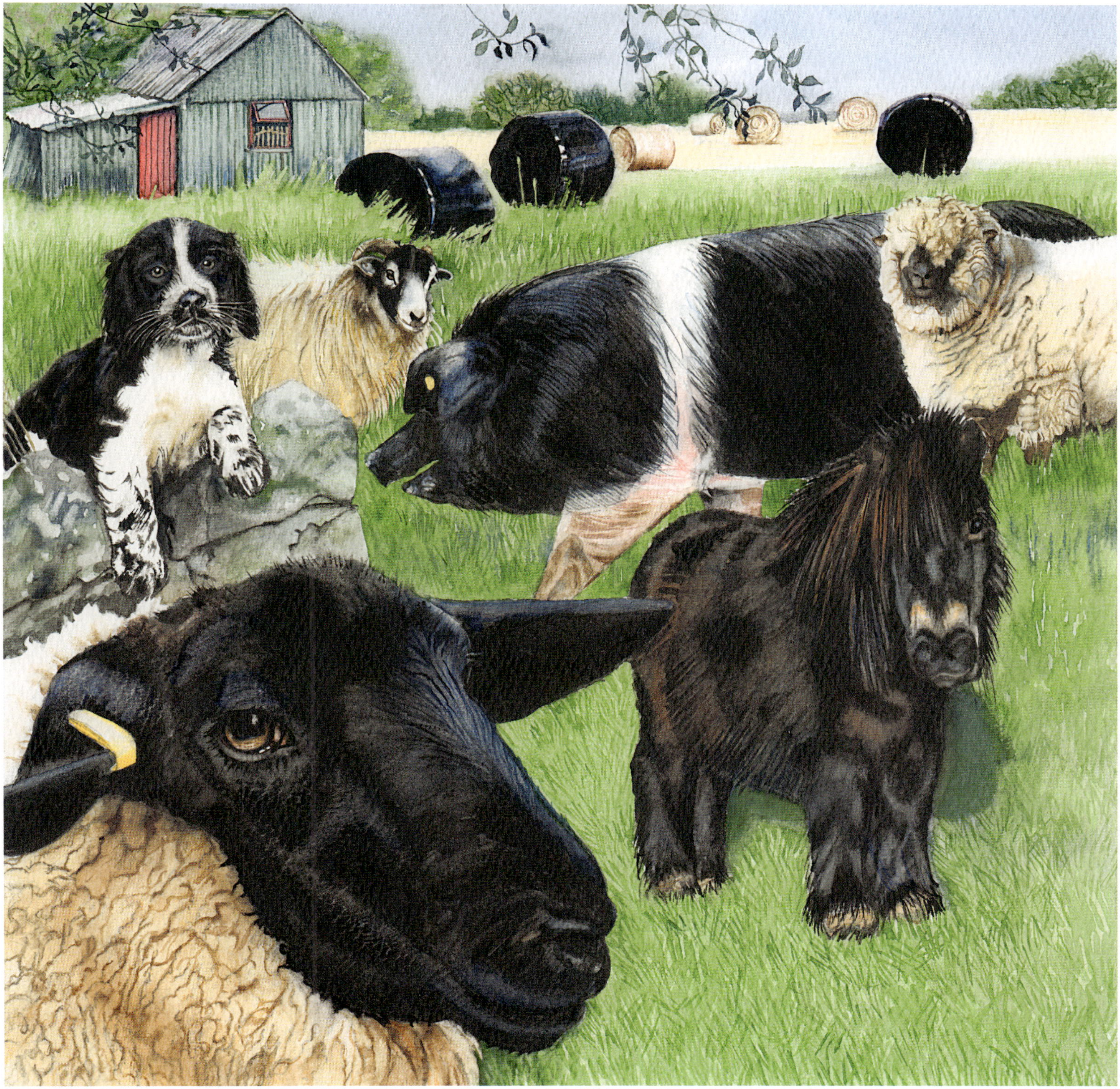

**T**exel **t**rio
**th**undering **th**oroughbreds
**tr**usty **T**amworth
**t**enacious **t**erriers
**T**illy **T**exel

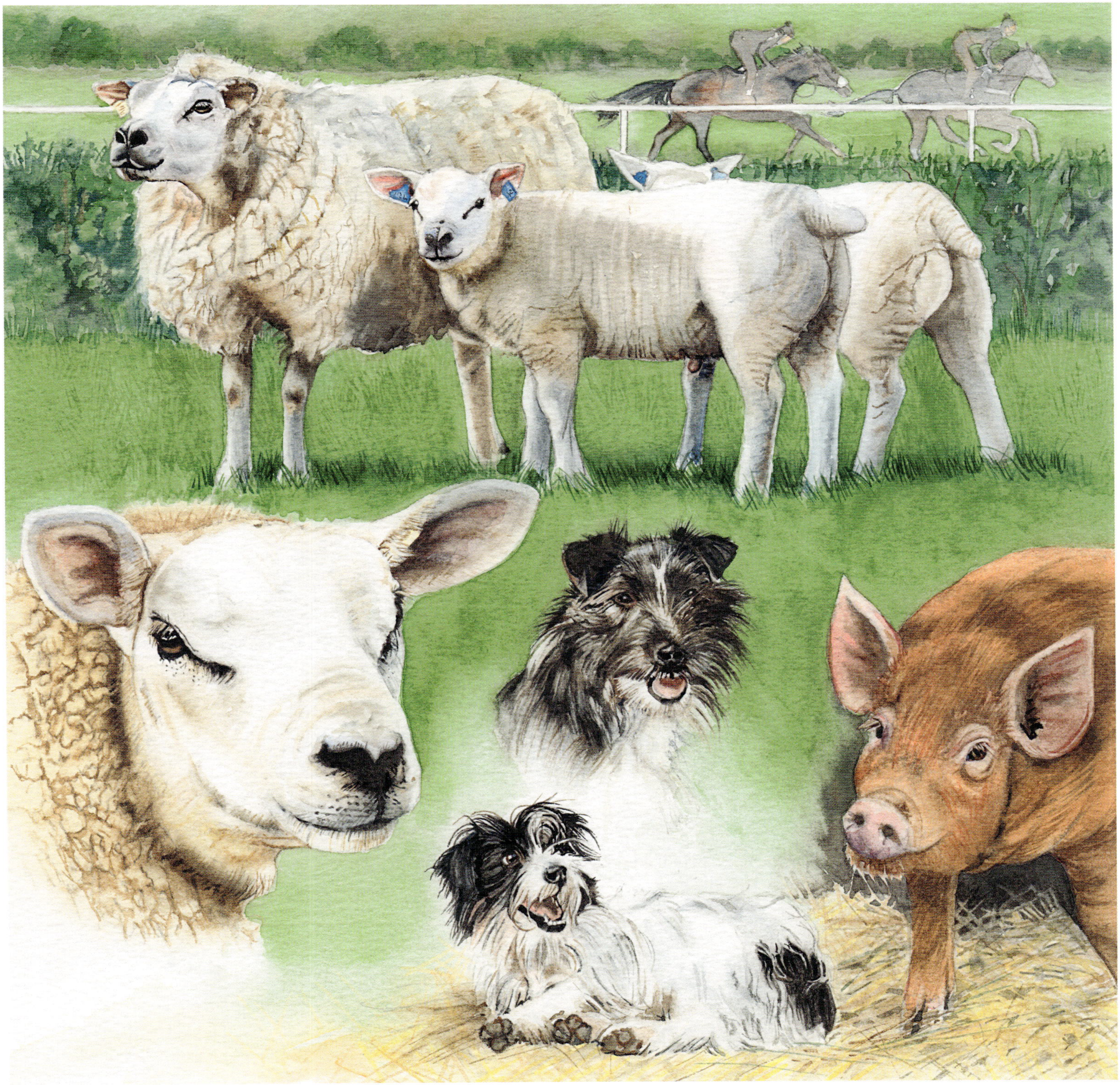

**u**nspoilt **u**plands
**u**psy-daisy
**u**phill
**u**mpteen **u**dders

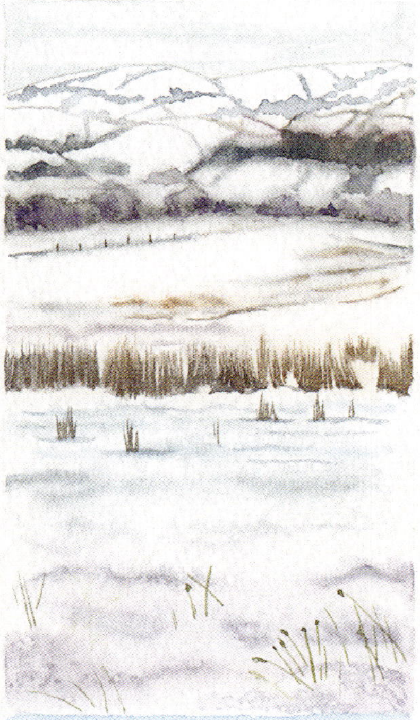

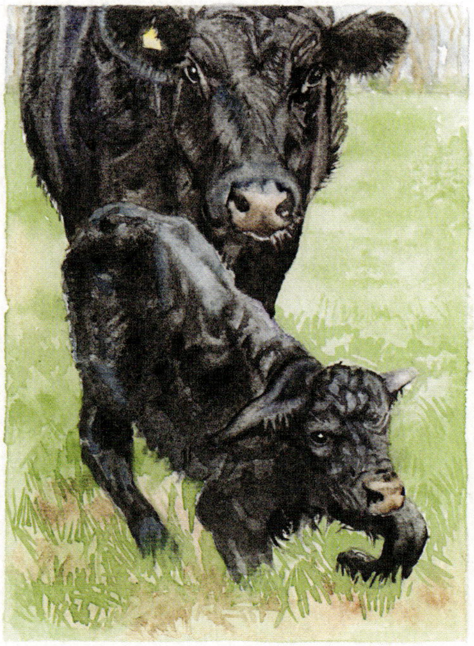

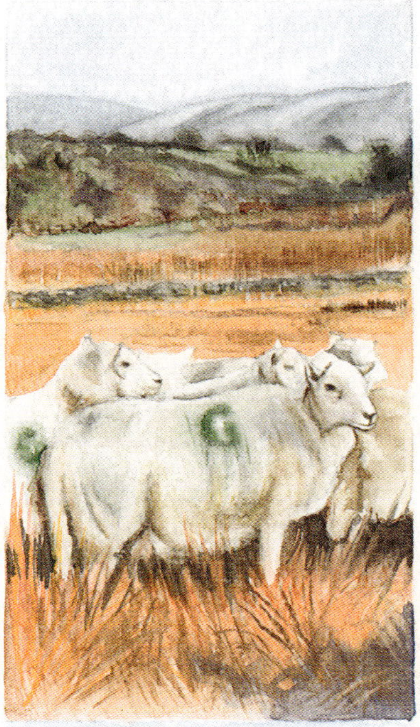

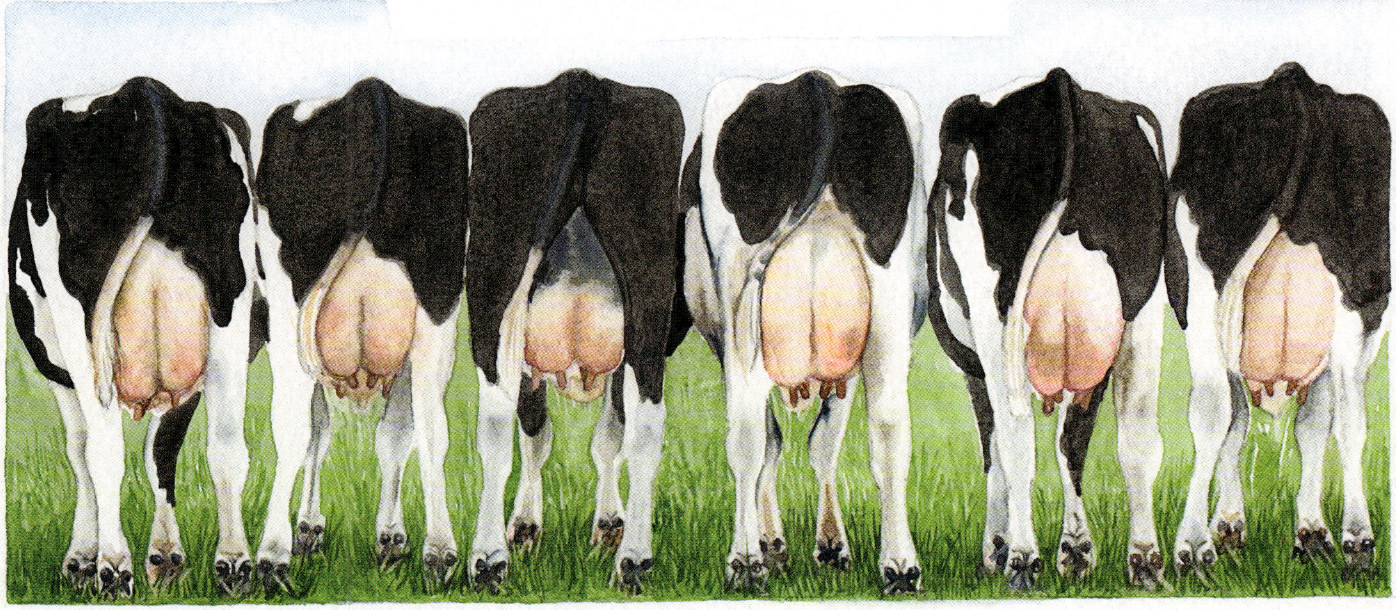

vigorous Vendeen

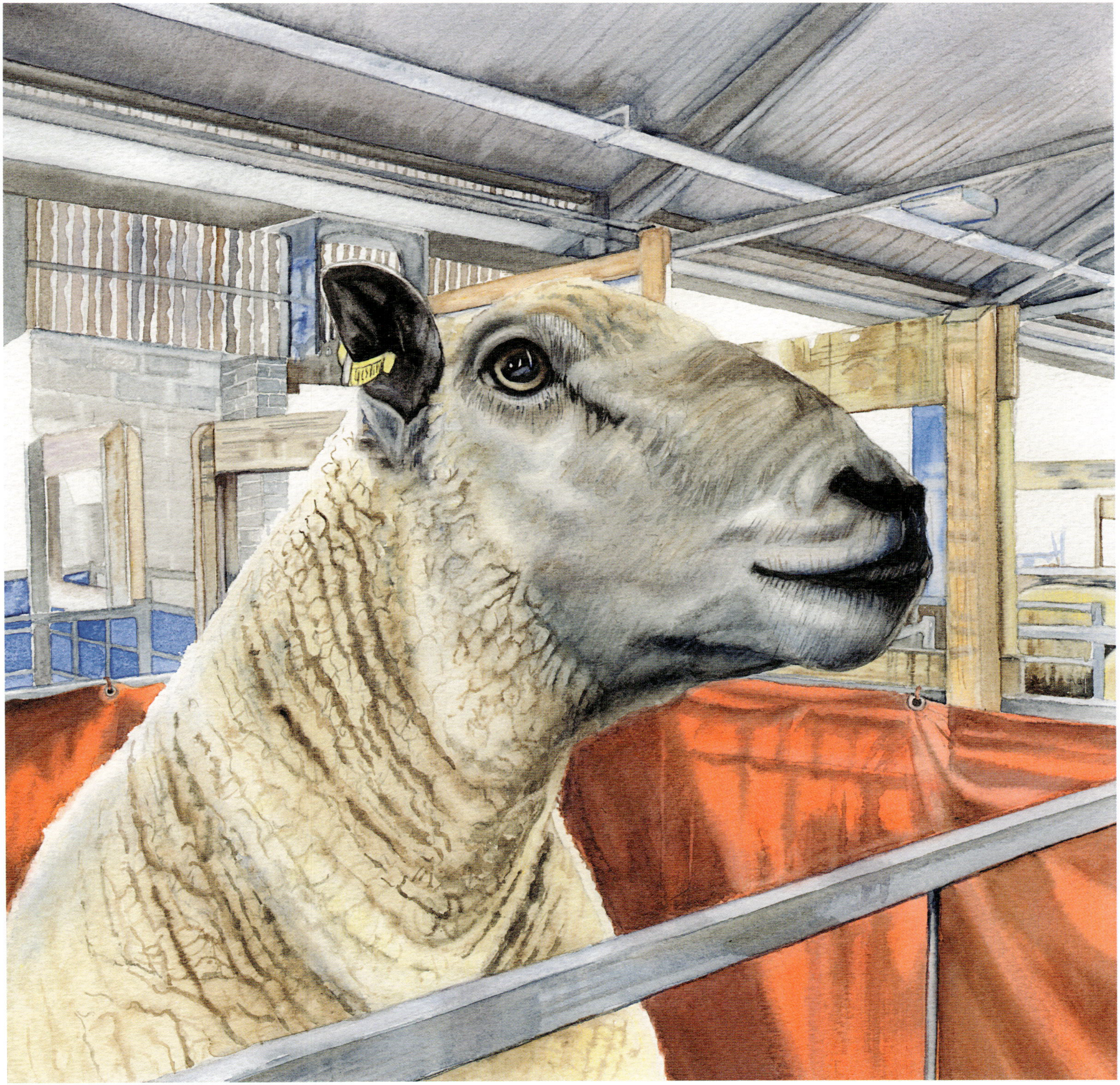

**w**onderful **W**elsh Cob
**w**inning **W**elsh Black
**w**hiskered **w**heat
**w**acky **W**ensleydale
**w**atchful **W**elsh Mountain
**w**ell-bred **W**iltshire Horn

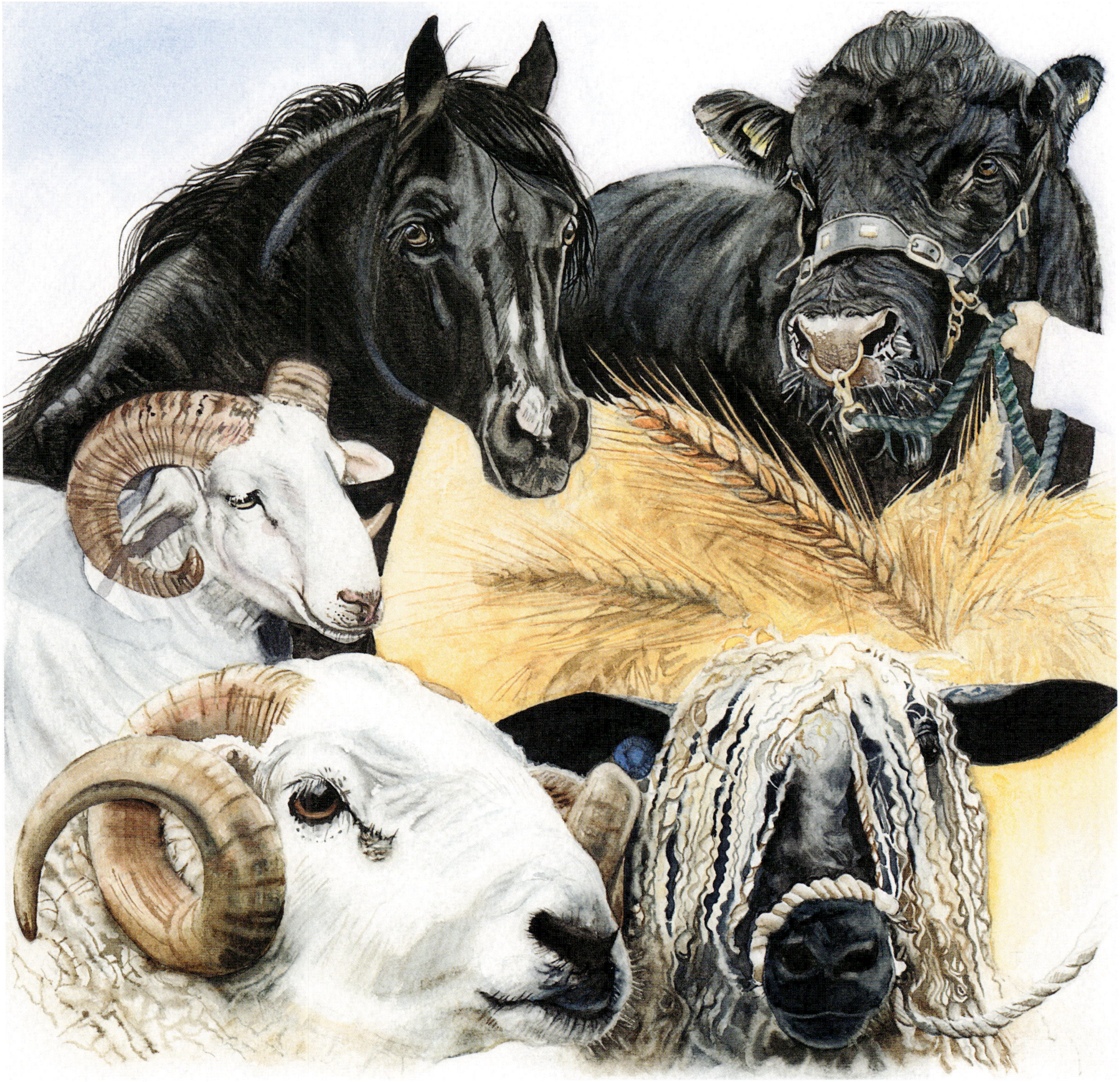

# X-ray

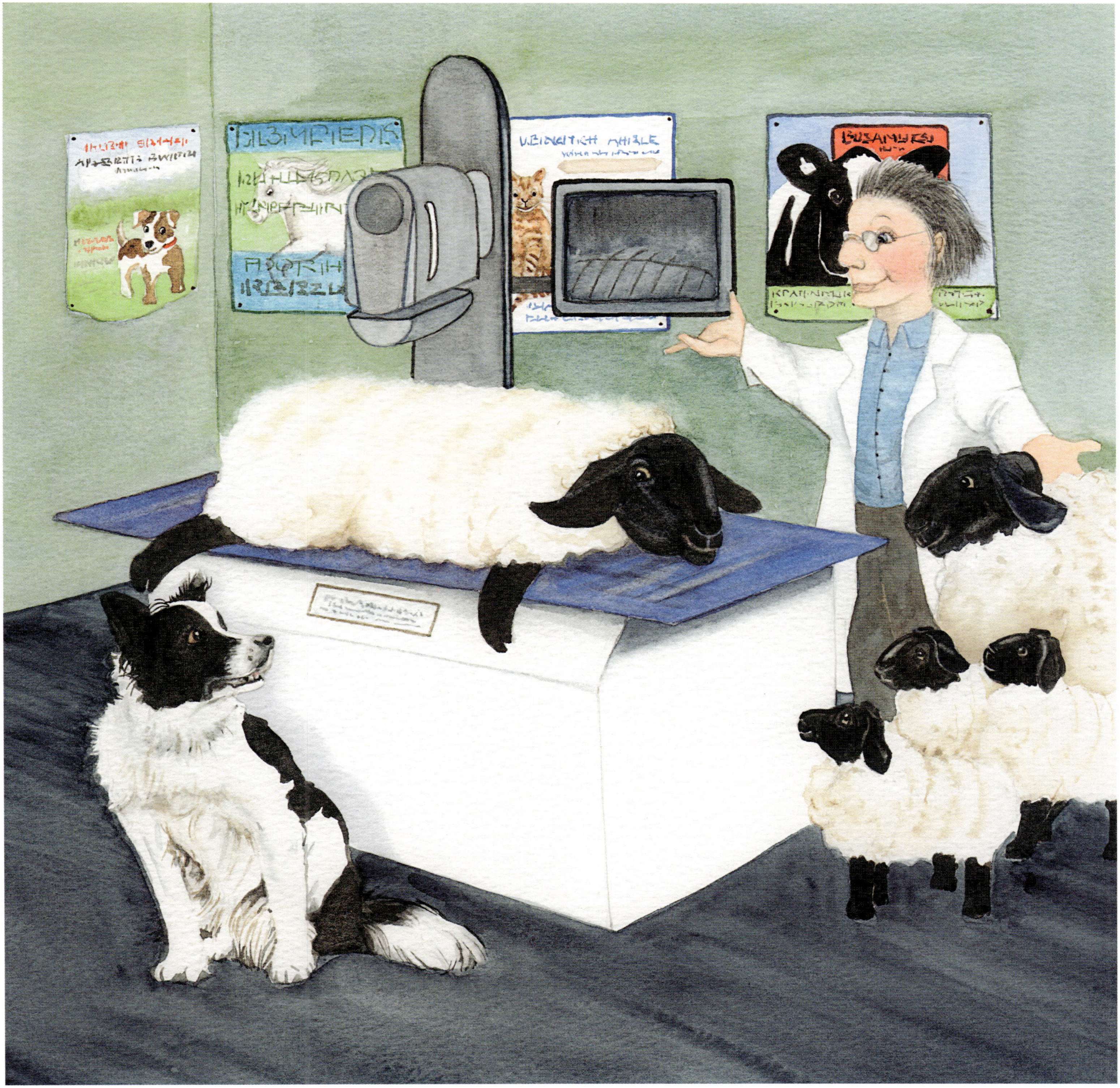

**Y**ew (and **y**onder **Y**ew)
**y**awning
**y**elping
**y**odelling
**y**apping

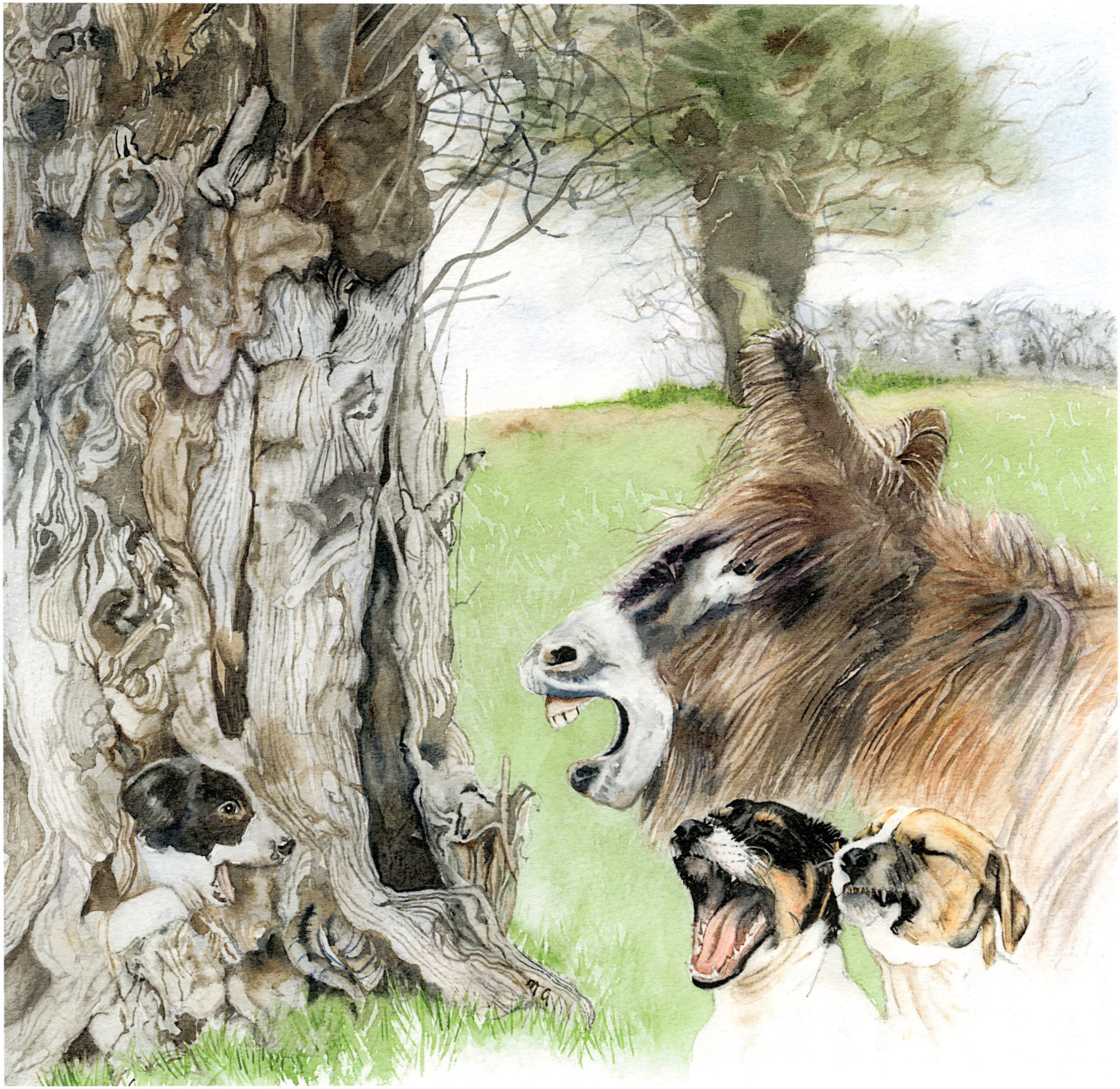

zany Zwartbles

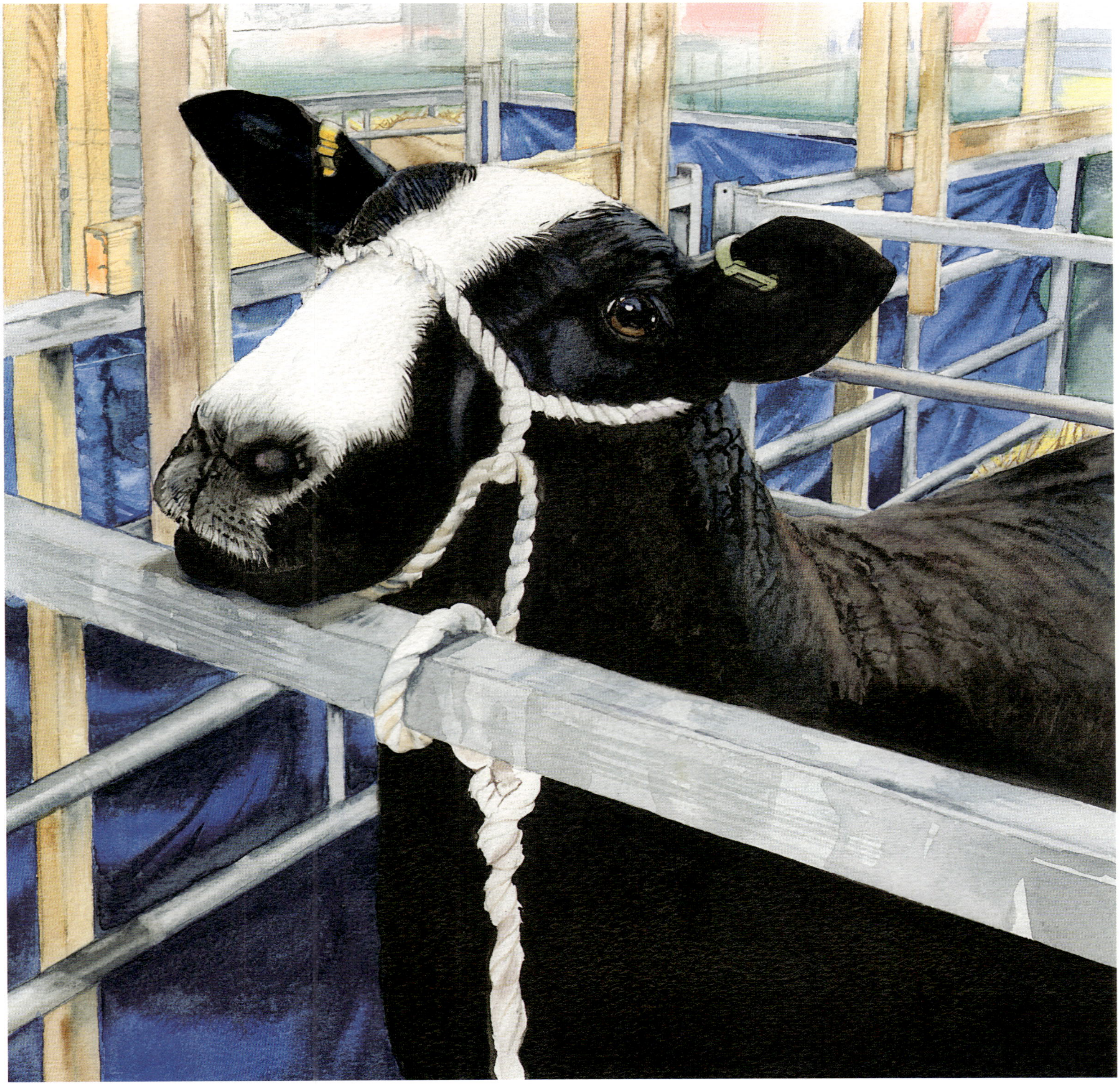

Mary Griese, 2014

Photograph by Janette Edmunds of Harptrees Photography